How To Learn Any Skill Fast

Quick Start Guide

I0482579

HTeBooks

Disclaimer

This book is designed to provide condensed information. It is not intended to reprint all the information that is otherwise available, but instead to complement, amplify and supplement other texts. You are urged to read all the available material, learn as much as possible and tailor the information to your individual needs.

Every effort has been made to make this book as complete and as accurate as possible. However, there may be mistakes, both typographical and in content. Therefore, this text should be used only as a general guide and not as the ultimate source of information. The purpose of this book is to educate.

The author or the publisher shall have neither liability nor responsibility to any person or entity with respect to any loss or damage caused, or alleged to have been caused, directly or indirectly, by the information contained in this book.

Table of Contents

How Will This Book Help You?

Think about all the things in life you've always wanted to do. Learn a language, ride a bike, climb Mount Everest. Everyone has a list of things they want to do and they usually put it in the back of their mental attics and label it 'maybe, someday, when I find the time.' Then after gathering a plethora of things to do, people end up sitting in front of the television or computer idling away their hours. They go about their days like this because deep down they know – or think they know – that they neither have the skill nor time to get these things done; but then again, deep down, they also know that they would like to learn how to.

What usually deters people from going out and learning all that they can is the perceived barriers to learning. They feel that they will be setting themselves up for frustration and failure. Ultimately they see it as a waste of time. This is indeed a reasonable concern. However, what is really gained without a little grit and hard work? Who can ignore the satisfaction of having learned something, from scratch no less? Wouldn't it be cool if you could do what you've always wanted to by learning quickly? Imagine the fun you could be having with a new set of skills.

Well, everyone starts out unskilled. Everyone has to realize this. Even some persons branded as prodigies had to learn skills to make use of or compliment their innate abilities. What everyone needs to know is there are less painful and frustrating ways of achieving what they want in the least time possible.

This book is precisely meant to help you do just that – make learning easier. It is not a 'learn how to....in a day' book, although it is quite possible to learn something in a day. Instead it is a guidebook to help you learn the smart and efficient way. Learning will not be instantaneous. However, it can be done considerably easier. This book is meant to help address two important concerns: time and skill. It will teach you how to manage your precious time so that you can learn skills that are fun and dear to you. Get to ride that bike, converse with people from different parts of the world, conquer that mountain you've always wanted to climb – fast! By simply managing how you think about learning, you can achieve quick results you did not even imagine was possible.

In this book, you will find a step-by-step checklist of principles. Each principle has its own chapter explaining how it will help you acquire skills you've always wanted in the least possible time. These are general principles that can be applied to any endeavor, big or small. By the end of this book, hopefully you will be transformed into a learning genius.

Finding a Project You Love

"The best thing that can happen to a human being is to find a problem, to fall in love with that problem, and to live trying to solve that problem, unless another problem even more lovable appears."

- Karl Popper

The first step to skill acquisition is not a complicated one. You simply have to find something that you love to do. This is an important part of the process because every skill is essentially a solution to a problem. So this means that skill acquisition involves finding a solution to a problem or point of difficulty. When trying to learn a skill, you can then expect to hit a lot of snags that can slow you down or ultimately make you quit. Loving the task at hand will lessen the frustration that comes along with learning a skill and solving problems.

Making mistakes will not sting as much if you enjoy what you're doing. You can just shrug it off and laugh. When you do make gains in learning the skill, it will be all the more satisfying. Ultimately, it will give you the impetus to work through the struggles and apply more effort. More effort and less frustration would translate to acquiring the skill faster.

Finding the suitable skill or activity for you is almost entirely personal. It mostly involves finding a balance between the enjoyment you will get out of the skill and the urgency or need for it. While nothing is wrong with learning a skill just for fun, nothing beats learning a fun skill because you know you can use it. Assess what your interests are and rank them. Now cross-reference this to which skills are useful to you at the moment. It is natural for you to learn higher ranking skills than lower ranking ones.

For example, you think that learning Italian would be cool. If it has been your life-long dream to learn it, then you will most likely learn it faster. Suppose that you've also wanted to learn Swedish and you also plan on taking a trip there in a few months. The added incentive of actually using the skill will give you more drive to learn Swedish faster than Italian. In fact, you might want to set aside the less useful skill for later.

Remember though that your interests and needs might change over time. So what is important and fun to you now can lose its appeal in the middle of the learning process. So you have to really want to learn something if you want to learn it rapidly.

Find a skill/project that you love, enjoy and can use.

Focusing On Your Skill

" Success demands singleness of purpose. You need to be doing fewer things for more effect instead of doing more things with side effects."

- Gary Keller

One pitfall of deciding to acquire skills is trying to do them all at once. The previous chapter touched upon the issue of having a hierarchy of several interests. You would choose one over the other because it appealed to you more. However, what happens when you can't decide which you like best? Most people would attempt to learn several things at once and end up with nothing.

This happens to be one of the problems of the formal education system: students are forced to learn several skills in a limited amount of time. The result is that they have to juggle things around. At the end of the semester or school year, they are left with no actual skills because they could not focus on just one due to the constraints of the system. You on the other hand, are not limited by the same constraints. You are not forced to learn several things at a time. You have the luxury of focusing on one skill at a time– so use it!

Remember that the goal is to acquire a skill in the least amount of time. So it is just logical for you to take things one at a time so that you can learn your desired skill faster. The more time and effort you put into other skills, the less time and effort you have for your desired skill. If you spread yourself too thin between several things, then you will waste too much energy on switching between skills. You will end up frustrated with one thing and move on to another. This will impede your learning and get you nowhere.

Focus is the name of the game if you want to learn really fast. Focused and deliberate effort on one skill will help you absorb information faster. Your brain is indeed capable of processing several things at one time, but if it gets too cluttered you will not gain much progress. You are trying to minimize impediments to learning and maximize your chances of acquiring your skill. If you really want to learn several skills, it would be better for you to pick one and list the rest of them down for now. You can tackle the others in the future, keeping in mind your level of interest and need for them.

Concentrate your effort on one skill at a time.

Setting Your Goals

"A problem well stated is a problem half solved."

- Charles Kettering

The next step in the process is to set your specific personal goal. Your general goal is to learn a skill. Your specific personal goal is what level of skill you want to acquire. You should be clear on what is good enough to you before you start. Otherwise, you would never know if you've accomplished what you set out to do. If you can tell yourself what you want to achieve, then the only problem left for you is achieving it.

You should be clear on what you will be able to do when you are done learning. The more specific you can make your goal, the easier and faster it is for you to reach. With this goal in mind, you can gauge whether or not you are actually getting closer to learning or if you have to use a few more hours of practice.

Defining your personal goal will usually depend on the reason why you want to learn the skill. If you are learning the skill just for kicks, then you should necessarily want to work at it until you lose the frustration and start having fun at it. If you intend to use the skill for something more serious, you should set your minimum level of performance. Once you reach your minimum goals, you can always choose to get better at the skill or you can cross it off the list and find another project to start.

Generally, the more relaxed your specific goal is, the faster you can acquire it. Remember, you are trying to be capable and sufficient as fast as possible; you are not trying to be the greatest master of the skill yet. You can get to that after. Right now you have to start from somewhere.

Another note on the matter would be thinking of your safety. Some skills have a measure of danger attached to them. Make sure you are aware of these dangers and sufficiently prepare for them. Include them in considering your specific goal. You do not want to hurt yourself in the process of learning.

Lastly, your goal will resonate all through the entire process of learning. It might help to write it down in a progress notebook or post it on your wall. This way, you can always refer back to it when in doubt.

Specify your goal – what you want to be able to do.

Breaking Things Down

"The secret of getting ahead is getting started. The secret of getting started is breaking your complex overwhelming tasks into small manageable tasks, and starting on the first one."

- Mark Twain

When you think of skills, you tend to imagine them as a single unit that you have to learn in its entirety. However, most of the things you label as skills usually consist of smaller parts or sub-skills. Take for example the skill of portrait painting. You would think that it is pretty straightforward: you pick up a brush and start painting things and people. In reality however, it entails many processes such as selecting the kind of medium, subject matter, kinds of brush strokes, color blending, and the like.

If you remember, in the second chapter, it was noted that when you try to learn several things at a time, you will most likely not learn anything at all. The same idea applies here. You should break down your desired skill and tackle each part to ensure focused learning. This keeps you from being overwhelmed by the amount of information you have to take in. You don't have to juggle all the parts in your mind. Instead, you can train your attention on what is at hand then move one to another when you are done.

More importantly, this allows you to see which parts of the skill are essential to beginners and which are better suited for experts. If you can isolate the critical portions of the skill, you can make more progress without being burdened by the less essential things. By stripping the learning program of things that are not important for the goal or performance level you set, you can cut down the time it takes for you to acquire your skill. As an added bonus, each segment of the skill you learn gives you the satisfaction of achieving something quicker. You would expect that each sub-skill can be learned faster than the entire skill itself. Enjoy learning each and you will compound the satisfaction of putting them all together.

Now, bring your attention back to the example of portrait painting. Suppose you set your goal as being able to do an accurate self-portrait in black and white based on photograph. Your goal is specific enough and allows you to cut out parts of the skill such as blending colors and painting moving subjects. Instead, you can prioritize learning sub-skills that are more essential to you, like shading and scaling.

Break your skill into sub skills and prioritize.

Finding the Right Tools

"If you ain't got no axe, you can't cut no wood."

- John Eaton

Most skills you want to learn need some tool or other resource for practicing or performance. If you want to try archery, then you would necessarily need a bow and a bunch of arrows, you can't shoot a basketball without a ball, and so on. Before you get to practicing, you need to know what implements are needed. Make a list of what you need now and will need in the future.

The main idea here is accessibility and convenience. You cannot effectively practice if you have to constantly spend time and effort in looking for things you that you could have prepared beforehand.

Take note of things that you already own. Look for what you can buy or borrow. See what your budget covers based on what you want to achieve. You can lose concentration and drive if you keep on thinking of expenses. More importantly, you can lose resources if you do not plan well, and that is not fun at all.

Cover all the bases so it will be smooth sailing when you start practicing. Remember that some skills do not only require tools, but also venues and environments. You need a skating rink if you want to learn ice skating. You also need a quiet place if you want to learn Chinese meditation techniques. Maximize your time spent training and practicing by having all you need at hand. If your skill has an element of hazard to it, then make sure that you take account for this. Find a practice area away from populated areas if necessary.

Know the things you need and prepare them.

Breaking Down the Barricades

"If you always put a limit on everything you do, physical or anything else. It will spread into your work and into your life. There are no limits. There are only plateaus, and you must not stay there, you must go beyond them."

- Bruce Lee

Several things can prevent you from effective practice and ultimately learning. These can be physical barriers in the form of lack of tools, misplacement of things and a disorderly workplace. The constant need to borrow what you need can also serve as an impediment. As stated in the previous chapter, you should make sure you have access to what you need when you need it. This saves you the effort and energy. It ultimately makes for smoother practice and faster learning.

You can also be distracted by external factors such as constant phone calls, television, social networking, and the like. Place yourself in an environment suitable for what you intend to do. Minimize unnecessary distractions that can make you lose momentum and take up precious learning time.

Emotional issues can also prevent you from learning effectively. You might be afraid or embarrassed to start working on your project. You may want to learn something, but it might be a bit dangerous or edgy. Make yourself comfortable by getting safety gear or finding assurance that you will not be hurt. If the activity seems awkward, do it with other people to make you comfortable that you are not doing it alone. Or you can always do it in the solitude of a secluded place so you will not fear ridicule while you are still getting the hang of things. Always keep in mind that you are trying to learn something you would love and enjoy. The satisfaction of acquiring a skill will always trump whatever misgivings you have. Have fun with the learning process and don't worry about failure. Laugh and shrug it off. The more relaxed you are in practicing, the easier it is for you to absorb what you are trying to learn.

You cannot always rely on willpower alone to overcome these barriers while you are practicing or training. You need to take care of these before you even start. Rearrange your surroundings to make it easy for you to begin. You cannot spare any time for distractions if you want to acquire your skills fast and effectively.

Remove all the barriers that prevent you from learning.

Making Time

"You will never find time for anything. If you want time, you must make it."

- Charles Buxton

The above quote is dead on when it comes to time. Most people tend to think that they can miraculously 'find time' in a day to practice. The reality is this never happens. If you do not set aside a certain part of your day for practice, then you will tend to waste hours just idling around. If you decide to learn a skill and you want to do it quick, then there is always the necessary trade-off of spending more time on it and less on other things. So this means it's time to cut down on some less important things like television, video games and surfing the net. The previous chapter already warned you about distractions from starting. Removing these unnecessary impediments will also work to eliminate delays in your skill acquisition.

A good tip is to take a notebook and log how you spend your day in hours. Once you do this, you can visualize your day and shuffle things around to make time. You can see where you waste time and where you can save it. Remember that you have twenty-four hours in a day. Eight of these hours are usually spent sleeping, which is important if you want effective retention of information and training. You are left with sixteen hours that you have to allocate between work and spending time with friends and family perhaps.

You should not neglect your responsibilities, of course. The time left from these activities has to be given to your practice and training. If you really want to learn as quickly as possible, then the trick is to allocate bigger blocks of time for practicing. Uninterrupted practice is always best and leads to better results. A good starting point is to allot at least an hour and a half a day for your practice.

It is also recommended that you commit yourself to do at least a total of twenty-four hours of practice. When you hit a snag, you should push on until you reach the target hours or your target goal. If you find that twenty-four hours seem to be too big an investment for your skill, maybe you should reassess if you really want to learn it. You can move on to another one and come back to it later. Pre-committing a definite amount of time will help you through the rough patches of early practice. You can expect that it will be hard at first and will be filled with frustration.

Setting a twenty-four hour goal gives you something to visualize and is helpful in maintaining your drive. You should look at this as an exercise in persistence. You should not let tiny hindrances stop you from doing what you set out to do. Once you hit the target number of hours, you can assess if you achieved your specific goal if you have not done so earlier. From there, you are in the proper position to decide whether you should keep on practicing or if you are ready to acquire a brand new skill.

Dedicate a definite amount of time to practice.

Finding Feedback

" I think it's very important to have a feedback loop, where you're constantly thinking about what you've done and how you could be doing it better. I think that's the single best piece of advice: constantly think about how you could be doing things better and questioning yourself. "

- Elon Musk

Getting feedback means getting information on whether or not you are doing well. Feedback is very important for learning because it is what tells you when progress is being made. Conversely, it also tells you when more work has to be put in. If you are doing well, carry on or do better. When you see that you messed up, make adjustments and try again.

If you want to gain a skill fast, your feedback also needs to return to you fast and accurate. The longer it takes for you to get feedback, the more time it will take for you to learn because it means more time to wait before you can make your adjustments. The time you can practically get feedback will vary greatly depending on the skill you want to learn.

If you are trying your hand at grafting ornamental plants, then you may not know when the graft is successful for a couple of weeks. However, if you want to learn ornamental pruning, you can immediately see the effects of your practice. You can compare diagrams with your work or you can even ask the neighbor or a local gardener if your work looks good. The best kind of feedback is the most immediate.

You can find feedback in several forms depending on your skill desired. You can find trainers, coaches or other experts who can mentor you while you practice. They are excellent sources of tips, tricks and feedback. For instance, a gym trainer can give you real-time feedback on your weightlifting form while you do it. If you prefer to do things solo, then you can also opt to use video capture of yourself practicing to help assess your progress. Part of your preparation in finding the right tools could include finding implements, measuring devices, computer programs or the like that can help you assess your progress. The more sources of feedback you can find and utilize, the faster you can learn your skill.

Remember that feedback has to be accurate as well. You will be wasting time if you kid yourself with biased and unreliable sources of feedback. You will end up with a big ego and no skill to show for it. Be honest with yourself and admit if you are not doing well so you can objectively assess your results.

Establish a fast and reliable feedback system.

Quick, Timed Practices

" What I have achieved by industry and practice, anyone else with tolerable natural gift and ability can also achieve."

- Johann Sebastian Bach

The early parts of practice will usually test your patience. You will probably feel like time is moving very slow and this will make you feel frustrated. Your mind is simply not wired to accurately tell time. This can lead to frustration and the feeling of fatigue even if you've only been practicing for a short period of time. This can make learning hard and near impossible at times.

The best way to remedy this is to time your practice sessions. Get a countdown timer, set it for say twenty to thirty minutes. Once you start the countdown, you need to practice until the time is up. No excuses. This way, you can stop worrying about time moving slowly. All you have to do is focus on practicing.

Let the timer worry about how long you have been at it. Repeat this over and over extending the countdown over time. This simple process will help you get used to practicing over longer periods of time and help you break through frustration and fatigue.

Doing a lot of these timed practice sessions will help you learn faster. You can set up as many as six of these in a day. Doing this will definitely get you great results in a short period of time with less frustration.

Practice in timed intervals and practice often.

Practicing a Lot

"I fear not the man who has practiced 10,000 kicks once, but I fear the man who has practiced one kick 10,000 times"

- Bruce Lee

When you are starting out, you will most likely be thinking that you have to practice perfectly. After all, they do say that 'perfect practice makes perfect'. However, you should remember that you are not trying to be a grandmaster of the skill just yet. Your goal is to learn the skill and be capable at it in the shortest possible time. Bruce Lee may have been a perfectionist. You are not aiming for perfection. Instead, you should take a leaf from his book when it comes to quantity of practice. Practice your kicks ten thousand times before you think of perfection.

The trouble with aiming for perfection at the onset is that it takes too much time even for a master at the skill. You can just imagine how long it will take for a beginner to do something perfectly without any training at all. Add to that the frustration that this can build up if you expect yourself to perform near perfectly when you are just starting. Keep in mind that you are just starting out, it is alright for you to start out awkwardly.

What is important for you now is to start practicing and practicing often. For rapid skill acquisition, quantity of practice trumps quality. The faster and more often you practice, the easier it is for your mind to pick up patterns and apply these to future sessions. Your mind is hardwired to work with repetition. The more you do something, the easier it will be for you to repeat it. Once you are familiar with the motion or activity, it will be simpler for you to make subtle adjustments to achieve your specific performance level goal.

This is not to say that you should not try to achieve good form when you practice, but this is best done after you have gotten in a few sessions to get used to the skill being practiced. The rule is that your first sessions should be focused on doing the activity or getting used to the motions. When you are familiar with it, try achieving or at least approximating your target level of skill. You can then speed up your training.

The more sessions and the faster you can do them, the quicker you will be able to progress. Of course don't forget the system of feedback you established, you cannot learn without knowing if you are actually improving. The bottom line is that you should not kill yourself over perfection when you are starting out. Focus first on getting more sessions in, progress will follow.

Practice and more practice: quantity of practice first, quality is for later.

How to Apply What You've Learned?

The principles given in these chapters are ideally meant to be followed step-by-step and speak mostly of preparation both physically and mentally for the process of learning new skills. They are made as general as possible to accommodate any skill you wish to learn. They may not all fit perfectly with everything you want to learn, but most will be essential to it. To help you apply these guidelines even better, you can take note of the broader ideas being espoused. This way, you can add to and tweak them to suit your needs.

First, we have the *principle of efficiency*. You should always think of how you can achieve better results through spending the least resources. Resources mean your time, effort, energy and even financial resources. Streamline the learning process so that you can get rid of what is unnecessary and focus on what is essential. You have already eliminated the physical and emotional distraction, what else is slowing you down? Is there anything peculiar to your skill that can be tweaked? You have already determined the core sub-skills, which sub-skill will make learning the others easier?

Second, there is the *principle of orderliness*. Take note of ways that you can structure your learning. An orderly process is always friendly to learning. If you plan your learning in such a way that is logical, you can be sure that you will learn much easier and faster. This is not limited to orderly planning either; you can also consider the orderliness of your practice area. Are your tools where they should be? Is your work area clean? Is it affecting your learning? Are you logging your hours in a proper way?

Third, you have the *principle of managing your expectations*. You cannot expect to learn something immediately. Set your expectations reasonably. This is the reason why you set a specific goal as to your level of skill. Do not feel bad if you do not achieve things right away or if things are taking too long. You can always go back to the checklist and see if there is something else you haven't considered. Rapid skill acquisition is about setting manageable skill goals.

Fourth, you should *stack the deck*. Part of your preparation should be to make sure you know as much about the skill you want to learn as possible. Learning should start even before you practice. Stack the decks in favor of getting the best possible result. Read books, watch online videos, visit exhibitions. This will make you familiar with the related ideas and concepts. If you do this, then you will lessen the 'I'm new to this' feeling and speed up progress.

Lastly, *have fun with it*! Learning is an enjoyable process. The principles given in the chapters are meant to take away the frustration and grief that comes with learning, but the experience in itself is fulfilling. Many find that frustrations are part of it. They love a challenge and are not afraid to fail. Having this attitude is very helpful in acquiring skills. Learn to love the process as much as the result. Again, you are not trying to kill yourself over a new skill. Be a learning-junkie, it is one step-closer to becoming a learning genius.

www.ingramcontent.com/pod-product-compliance
Lightning Source LLC
Chambersburg PA
CBHW070310190526
45169CB00004B/1572